CANADIAN

With thanks to the
Metropolitan Toronto Police
and to Judge
Donna Hackett

P.B.

With thanks to the RCMP
Sechelt Detachment
and
for my Dad PC 260 LaFave (Ret.)

K.L.

Kids Can Press Ltd. acknowledges with appreciation the assistance of the Canada Council
and the Ontario Arts Council in the production of this book.

CANADIAN CATALOGUING IN PUBLICATION DATA

Bourgeois, Paulette
Canadian police officers

(In my neighbourhood)
ISBN 1-55074-060-1 (bound) ISBN 1-55074-133-0 (pbk.)

1. Police – Canada – Juvenile literature.
I. LaFave, Kim. II. Title. III. Series: Bourgeois, Paulette. In my neighbourhood.

HV8157.B68 1992   j363.2'0971   C91-095196-9

Stay Alert Stay Safe rules appearing on pages 30-32 are reproduced with the permission of
Stay Alert Stay Safe Organization © 1992

Kids Can Press Ltd.
29 Birch Avenue
Toronto, Ontario, Canada
M4V 1E2

Designed by N.R. Jackson
Typeset by Cybergraphics Co. Inc.
Printed and bound in Hong Kong by Everbest Co., Ltd.

PA 93 0 9 8 7 6 5 4 3 2 1

CANADIAN
POLICE OFFICERS

In My Neighbourhood

Paulette Bourgeois

Kim LaFave

KIDS CAN PRESS LTD.
Toronto

Everybody is asleep.

"Clank, clang, clatter, bang!"

Natalie hears the commotion and she's worried. Somebody has been stealing bicycles in the neighbourhood. Maybe the thieves are in her garage! Natalie creeps into her parents' room and whispers, "Call the police."

Natalie's mother reaches for the phone —
the police number is written clearly nearby.
When the phone is answered, she says, "We
think somebody is trying to break in. Our
name is Best. We live at 123 Main Street. The
closest intersection is Main and South streets."

"Don't worry," she tells Natalie. "The police
will be right here."

As soon as the police dispatcher gets the call, a message is sent to the computer or radio inside the patrol car closest to the Best's house.

Usually, the officers work in pairs at night. As soon as they hear the message, the officers signal to the dispatcher that they are on the way. In some emergencies, lots of police cars are sent. The officers do not use their siren this time — they want to arrive quietly and catch the thieves in action.

The officers use their flashlights to search the neighbourhood. A garbage can has been knocked over but there is no sign that somebody has tried to break open doors or windows. They jot in their notebooks and keep on looking.

"All quiet now," they tell the Best family. "There have been a lot of bicycle thefts around here. Do you have a good lock on your bike?" they ask. Natalie nods. "And I know the make, the colour and the registration number," she says.

"That's smart!" say the officers. "Sometimes we find lost or stolen bicycles and we don't know who owns them."

On the way to school, Natalie notices something suspicious. There is a big blue van parked behind an abandoned building. She writes the licence plate number in her notebook and tells the principal when she gets to school. The principal calls the police.

The officers drive slowly by the schoolyard. At the bike rack, they see two men look around nervously and then, in a flash, slice through a bicycle lock with a small saw.

Just as they are about to ride off, the police officers tell them they are under arrest for stealing, and they are going for a different ride — to the police station.

At the station, the men are questioned. Lawyers and senior police officers make sure the men are treated properly. The police officers who made the arrest still have work to do. They look in the back of the blue van — there are 15 bicycles inside!

The men are let go until their trial in a court-room. In court, a lawyer for the accused men and a lawyer for the government, who is called a Crown Attorney, will ask the police officers questions about what they saw. It will be the judge's job to decide if the men are guilty of stealing bicycles and, if they are, to decide on a punishment.

Later that night, Natalie hears "Clank, clang, clatter, bang!"

"The bike thieves are back!" she calls to her parents. "Call the police!"

The officers arrive within seconds. They move quickly and quietly through the dark. They shine their flashlights into the alley.

"I've caught the masked robbers," says the officer. "But I think we'll let them go with a warning."

A police officer has to be prepared for anything.

All police officers are ready to help people who
are lost, hurt or afraid. They are your friends.
The police make sure people obey the law.
And there are many different kinds of police
work. Some officers teach children to be safe.

Some officers control the crowds at concerts and sports events.

Some officers investigate crimes and traffic accidents.

There are different kinds of police. Many towns, cities, provinces, territories and native communities have their own police forces. The Royal Canadian Mounted Police work all across Canada. The RCMP wear their "dress-up" clothes — bright red uniforms and brown hats — for special jobs such as performing in the Musical Ride or guarding the entrance to Canada's Parliament Buildings.

Mostly, the RCMP wear a regular uniform when they do their police work.

Some police officers walk in the neighbourhood and get to know all the people in their
community. But the police get around in lots of
different ways:

in a van

in a helicopter

on a motorcycle

in a boat

on a bicycle

in a patrol car.

Police officers are physically fit. They are not too short and not too tall. They must have good eyesight. Police officers have revolvers but they hope they never have to use them.

Sometimes officers wear
bullet-proof vests. They
carry notebooks and hand-
cuffs and wear a belt with
a night stick and a flashlight.

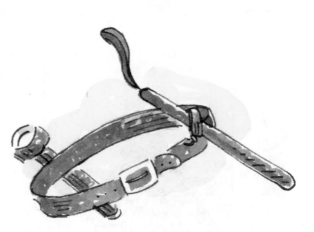

Remember to Stay Alert and
Stay Safe

Always stick with the same route for
going to and from school, playgrounds
and friends' homes. Make sure
your parents know the routes
you take. Check the route
over with a parent for
possible unsafe places.

Always stay away from
lonely parks, woods,
parking lots and school-
yards late after school.

Always go places with bud-
dies and make sure your parents know where you are at
all times. Keep your friends'
addresses and phone num-
bers by your phone.

Always say "No" if anybody
invites you alone into his or
her home or car — even if
you're with friends.

Always tell your parent or an adult you trust if something has happened that bothers you, even if it is about somebody your family knows well and likes. It's not your fault if somebody acts in a way that makes you uncomfortable. You don't have to keep it a secret no matter what anyone says.

Always keep the door closed and locked when you are home alone.

Always pretend you've got grown-up company if you're home alone.

Always have a family password. Adults who want you to stay with them, or go somewhere with them, must know the password.

Always refuse to go anywhere with a stranger or somebody who makes you feel uncomfortable — no matter what they say to you. Most people are helpful and kind, but some people are mean. They might try to trick you by offering you something nice such as a kitten, a puppy, a toy or an ice-cream. They might try to trick you by telling you that something is wrong with your parents. They might even trick you by telling you that you are going to be on a television show or made famous if you go with them.

Never go anywhere with a stranger.